8 HEAVENLY FOCUSED WORK HABITS

MW01670771

INSPIRATIONS FROM PSALM 37

8 HEAVENLY FOCUSED WORK HABITS

MEL HIBBARD

TATE PUBLISHING
AND ENTERPRISES, LLC

Eight Heavenly Focused Work Habits
Copyright © 2013 by Mel Hibbard. All rights reserved.

No part of this publication may be reproduced, stored in a retrieval system or transmitted in any way by any means, electronic, mechanical, photocopy, recording or otherwise without the prior permission of the author except as provided by USA copyright law.

Scripture quotations marked (KJV) are taken from the *Holy Bible, King James Version*, Cambridge, 1769. Used by permission. All rights reserved.

The opinions expressed by the author are not necessarily those of Tate Publishing, LLC.

Published by Tate Publishing & Enterprises, LLC
127 E. Trade Center Terrace | Mustang, Oklahoma 73064 USA
1.888.361.9473 | www.tatepublishing.com

Tate Publishing is committed to excellence in the publishing industry. The company reflects the philosophy established by the founders, based on Psalm 68:11,
"The Lord gave the word and great was the company of those who published it."

Book design copyright © 2013 by Tate Publishing, LLC. All rights reserved.
Cover design by Lindsay Behrens
Interior design by Caypeeline Casas

Published in the United States of America

ISBN: 978-1-62510-497-7
1. Religion / Christian Life / Professional Growth
2. Self-Help / Personal Growth / Success
13.02.07

DEDICATION

To the next generation
and my grandchildren—Jacob, Emma,
Conner, Ryan, Anna, and Thomas.

ACKNOWLEDGMENT

A special thanks to my wife, Deanna, and my family for their support and encouragement.

Tate Publishing and my editor, Hannah Tranberg, have been a great assistance also.

TABLE OF CONTENTS

INTRODUCTION

How are the ideas presented in these pages any different than those taught in a typical adult education?

You just need to reach down within yourself and pull yourself up by your bootstraps. Over thirty-plus years of adult education, whether a one-day seminar or several weeks of training, have taught me the answer to self-improvement is you. You make the adjustment that is needed, improve your weaknesses, and grow your strengths. However, as believers, we have a truth that goes way beyond man's understanding. All we need to do is follow the wisdom of Proverbs 3:6, "In all your ways acknowledge Him and He shall direct thy path." In all your ways, work, friends, home, church, recreation, etc., no matter what we are doing, we need to let the Lord control our ways. Living by those words is a lifelong commitment that is never taught in typical adult education.

These truths are from the Bible?

No doubt, the Bible has the answers to the way we should conduct ourselves as we deal with one another, whether at work, home, school, playground, or even church. I have often challenged Sunday school students to find answers to their social or peer pressure issues by searching the Word of God. By diligently searching the Bible, they find the answers to each and every issue. No matter what life's path, the correct direction to go can be found in the Bible.

Shortly before graduating from high school, I asked my dad if he thought I should become a missionary or engineer. He gave me some of the best advice ever, "That is something you have to get the answer from the Lord." I read and reread the book of Proverbs. I keyed in on Proverbs 3:5, 6: "Trust in the Lord with all thine heart; and lean not unto thine own understanding. In all thy ways acknowledge Him, and he shall direct thy path." That started me on the path that would lead to Eight Heavenly Focused Work Habits.

No matter the problem we face in life, the answer can be found in the Bible?

Those verses became the key to unlocking the answer to what the Lord wanted me to do with my life. No, he did not give me an audio answer or write something on the wall to let me know his will. Instead, he gave Solomon, the wisest man that ever lived, these words for me to read and start to understand as a teenager. At that age, I understood that putting my trust in him at the age of ten and giving myself to him

Did I just hear some bells and whistles from heaven?

You mean I have to take my hands of the steering wheel?

at age fourteen was the start of living my life with him as the driver.

With the Lord as the driver, we do not always know which direction he will take us at the intersection of life's crossroads. However, he does promise to direct our path if we fully trust and acknowledge him. He has also promised that he will provide our every need along the way (Matthew 6:33).

While I was attending Bible Club camp at the age of ten, the speaker gave a clear message on why Jesus Christ had once come to earth to pay the penalty for my sin and would return a second time for me if I asked for forgiveness of my sin and accepted his free gift (Romans 6:23). I went forward to be counseled and accepted Christ as my Savior that night. Four years later at the teen version of the same camp a missionary lady challenged the campers to dedicate their lives to living for Christ. I felt the Spirit touching my heart and told Him I would do whatever He wanted with my life in order to follow Him.

Paul said in his writing in Romans 12:1-2, "Therefore, I urge you, brothers, in view of God's mercy, to offer your bodies as living sacrifices, holy and pleasing to God—this is your spiritual act of worship. Do not conform any longer to the pattern of this world, but be transformed by the renewing of your mind. Then you will be able to test and approve what God's will is—his good, pleasing and perfect will." This tells us that it is only reasonable that believers should be a living sacrifice back to Jesus for what he did for us. Paul finishes by stating that as we have dedicated our lives to God's service, we can and should live in His will not our own.

Being a sacrifice involves following Christ's teaching instead of following the way of the world. The transformation that needs to take place in our lives involves letting Christ take control of the wheel all the time. This change in our life means putting on the whole armor of God as we are taught in Ephesians 6:10-20.

What is a good soldier?

To be in the center of God's will is a lifelong battle. Like good soldiers we need to be ready at all times to fight the battle. Jesus teaches us in Luke 9:23, "Then he said to them all: 'If anyone would come after me, he must deny himself and take up his cross daily and follow me.' We must surrender our lives each day and follow Him. This should remind us that it is no longer us but Christ that lives in us.

It all boils down to three decisions that will determine how we live our lives and our eternal destination:

1. Accept Christ as our Savior
2. Turn over (dedicate) our lives to Him
3. Take up our cross each day and follow Him

With these three decisions as our foundation, God has promised to give us the desires of our heart (which is now in tune with His). The thirty-seventh chapter of Psalms was penned by David and expands on what Solomon said in Proverbs 3:5, 6 and is the foundation of the eight work habits that are discussed in the following chapters. The italicized words of Psalms 37 that follows are the key phases that are discussed in this book.

1 Do not fret because of evildoers,
Nor be envious of the workers of iniquity.
2 For they shall soon be cut down like the grass,
And wither as the green herb.

3 *Trust* in the LORD, and *do good*;
Dwell in the land, and feed on His faithfulness.
4 Delight yourself also in the LORD,
And He shall give you the desires of your heart.

5 *Commit* your way to the LORD,
Trust also in Him,
And He shall bring it to pass.
6 He shall bring forth your righteousness as the light,
And your justice as the noonday.

7 Rest in the LORD, and *wait patiently for Him*;
Do not fret because of him who prospers in his way,
Because of the man who brings wicked schemes to pass.
8 *Cease from anger*, and forsake wrath;
Do not fret—*it* only causes harm.

9 For evildoers shall be cut off;
But those who wait on the LORD,
They shall inherit the earth.
10 For yet a little while and the wicked shall be no more;
Indeed, you will look carefully for his place,
But it shall be no more.
11 But the meek shall inherit the earth,
And shall *delight themselves in the abundance of peace.*

12 The wicked plots against the just,
And gnashes at him with his teeth.
13 The Lord laughs at him,
For He sees that his day is coming.
14 The wicked have drawn the sword
And have bent their bow,
To cast down the poor and needy,
To slay those who are of upright conduct.
15 Their sword shall enter their own heart,
And their bows shall be broken.

16 A little that a righteous man has
Is better than the riches of many wicked.
17 For the arms of the wicked shall be broken,
But the LORD upholds the righteous.

18 The LORD knows the days of the upright,
And their inheritance shall be forever.
19 They shall not be ashamed in the evil time,

And in the days of famine they shall be satisfied.
20 But the wicked shall perish;
And the enemies of the LORD,
Like the splendor of the meadows, shall vanish.
Into smoke they shall vanish away.

21 The wicked borrows and does not repay,
But the righteous shows mercy and gives.
22 For those blessed by Him shall inherit the earth,
But those cursed by Him shall be cut off.

23 The steps of a good man are ordered by the LORD,
And He *delights in his way*.
24 Though he fall, he shall not be utterly cast down;
For the LORD upholds him with His hand.

25 I have been young, and now am old;
Yet I have not seen the righteous forsaken,
Nor his descendants begging bread.
26 He is ever merciful, and lends;
And his descendants are blessed.

27 Depart from evil, and *do good*;
And dwell forevermore.
28 For the LORD loves justice,
And does not forsake His saints;
They are preserved forever,
But the descendants of the wicked shall be cut off.

29 The righteous shall inherit the land,
And dwell in it forever.

30 The *mouth of the righteous speaks wisdom*,
And his tongue talks of justice.
31 The *law of his God is in his heart*;
None of his steps shall slide.

32 The wicked watches the righteous,
And seeks to slay him.
33 The LORD will not leave him in his hand,
Nor condemn him when he is judged.

34 Wait on the LORD,
And keep His way,
And He shall exalt you to inherit the land;
When the wicked are cut off, you shall see it.
35 I have seen the wicked in great power,
And spreading himself like a native green tree.
36 Yet he passed away, and behold, he was no more;
Indeed I sought him, but he could not be found.

37 Mark the blameless man, and observe the upright;
For *the future of that man is peace*.
38 But the transgressors shall be destroyed together;
The future of the wicked shall be cut off.

39 But the salvation of the righteous is from the Lord;
He is their strength in the time of trouble.
40 And the Lord shall help them and deliver them;
He shall deliver them from the wicked,
And save them,
Because they trust in Him.

SETTING GOALS WITH CHRIST AT THE CENTER

PSALMS 37:3–5

Get the job done faster than the next guy?

Each and every year from 1981 until my retirement in 2010, I had to set goals for what I would accomplish during each and every calendar year. The results of those goals typically determined the raise in salary that would be earned whether working as a supervisor, coordinating multimillion dollar projects, or simply doing the mundane day-to-day tasks. I was always determined to get the job done faster than the guy next to me. Early in my career, at a yearly review, I got a satisfactory result. I asked the supervisor what I needed to do to get a satisfactory-plus review. He gave me a couple simple suggestions, and the next year I was happy to get that satisfactory-plus review.

What can I do to provide a better product?

From that time on, I always let the eighteen different supervisors that I had know that my goal was to exceed any goals set for me so that I would get at least a satisfactory-plus review. In fact, I asked them to let me know that if at any time during the year I was not exceeding those goals that they let me know. With only a couple of exceptions, this worked to my supervisor's satisfaction and my own as I exceeded those yearly goals.

All it takes is a little trust and commitment?

So what does that have to do with setting goals with Christ at the center? Pslams 37:3–5 states, "Trust in the LORD, and do good; so shalt thou dwell in the land, and verily thou shalt be fed. Delight thyself also in the LORD: and he shall give thee the desires of thine heart. Commit thy way unto the LORD; trust also in him; and he shall bring it to pass." In these three verses are two promises that deal with life's most important goals. Simply stated, we must first trust him and then commit. God does not just want us to trust him for what he has promised, our daily bread, but he wants us to commit our every move to him, and he will give us the desires of our heart.

We get the desires of our heart?

Wow, the desires of our heart—a fancy home, a new sports car every year, a motor home, a cabin on the lake, money to burn, endless vacations, a spouse that the world envies, a great family, in fact we should become the envy of the neighborhood. Romans 12:1, 2 gives us even more insight to what the desires of our heart should be: "I beseech you therefore, brethren, by the mercies of God, that ye present your bodies a living sacrifice, holy, acceptable unto God, which is your reasonable service. And be not conformed to this world: but be ye transformed by the renewing of your mind, that ye may prove what is that good, and acceptable, and perfect, will of God." Once we have turned our life completely over to Christ, his desires become our desires, and his goals become our goals. A totally transformed life is seldom seen in today's age of "me, mine, and my." But God's Word is very clear in that "me" has to die (living sacrifice) if we want to do his will.

What is the desire of His heart?

That commitment to fully turn over one's self to him gives him delight. His promise to us is that the desires of our heart will reflect his will. Sounds a little like double talk, but remember why he created us. If we put all of our work for the Lord in two words, they would simply be glorify him. John 15:7, 8 states, "If ye abide in me, and my words abide in you, ye shall ask what ye will, and it shall be done unto you. Herein is my Father glorified, that ye bear much fruit; so shall ye be my disciples." Jesus's own words tell us that we need to become one with him. He also tells us to forget about ourselves each and every day. Luke 9:23 states, "And he said to them all, If any man will come after me, let him deny himself, and take up his cross daily, and follow me." Whatever we do from the time we get up in the morning until we lose consciousness at the

Is it okay to have corporate goals?

end of the day needs to be done to glorify him.

So did he fulfill the teenage desires of my heart, such as a wife for life, a great family including grandkids, ways to serve him, a well-paying job, a nice home, a chance to be the best in one area of my job? Absolutely. Did everything go without bumps and any curves in the road? Absolutely not. But I have been blessed with three great kids that came to know Jesus as their personal savior before they were teens. And now, my desire is that all six grand kids can know that joy also. I have had a career that included several promotions and almost always had more in my pocket than I needed to pay the bills. At least three different times in my career, I was considered the expert go-to person that could help get answers to some of their problems.

Early in my career at the electric and gas utility, I had set goals of becoming a resident engineer by the time I was thirty-five, and my dream job of operating superintendent by the time I was forty. I did make resident engineer at age thirty-five and operating superintendent at age forty-one. At the age of forty-two, the company reorganized, and I spent one long weekend without that dream job after being told I was no longer the operating superintendent.

Is it okay to enjoy your job?

It was a tough weekend for my family and me, but I remember trusting that the Lord would supply all of our needs. By Tuesday, I had been reassigned a new job. The next six years, I spent in the corporate office becoming an expert in a couple different areas that continued to give me job satisfaction. I was truly blessed as I was able to enjoy the vast majority of my career. After getting my dream job, I thought that all of my career desires had been fulfilled at age forty-two. The next seventeen years were just as exciting as the first seventeen. Putting Christ first made all the difference as He fulfilled those promises.

Along the way, the Light has shown as we are told to do in Matthew 5:16: "Let your light so shine before men, that they may see your good works, and glorify your Father which is in heaven." Our family moved five different times, and in each location, I have had numerous opportunities to serve him. I have almost always taught Sunday school from toddlers to adults, serving him as deacon, trustee, Sunday school superintendent, doing carpentry or electrical work, singing in the choir, or sweeping the floors.

When we put Christ first, He will give us the desires of our heart.

Part of my life goals and the desire of my heart was to retire from work and be able to travel in a motor home and do work for Habitat for Humanity or a similar organization.

Well, a couple years ago, the utility company made me an offer I could not refuse, and I retired a couple years earlier than I had planned. I had numerous projects to do, including replacing the front and back decks and putting on new house siding. By midsummer, I had the list whittled down to just a few smaller projects. One of those small projects was to wire an outlet from the house so our motor home could be utilized for company and to keep the batteries

What if suddenly your plan takes a turn?

charged. I completed that project a few days before we were scheduled to go on a family camping vacation. Unfortunately or fortunately, the wiring was wrong and caused some problems in the motor home that could not be repaired before our camping trip.

A couple weeks earlier, we had been looking at upgrading the motor home, and my wife found a unit that was six years newer than the one we had. We both liked the additional features in this newer model. However, we did not want to go into debt to get a newer model, especially at the price we were quoted.

How come it is not going the way I thought it would?

How can this be good? How does the Lord give us the desires of our heart? How can all things work together for good? Romans 8:28 states, "And we know that all things work together for good to them that love God, to them who are the called according to his purpose." Two days later my oldest grandson and I were swapping motor homes in time for our yearly family camping trip. Of course, we now had a monthly payment that we were not planning to have during our retirement years. But by this time in my life I realized the truth of His promise in Romans 8:28 and knew He would provide. Indeed He did provide beyond my expectations.

Shortly after returning from our family vacation with the new motor home, I got a call from a previous coworker asking if I would like to do some contract work for the electric company for a few months. After getting the details, I said sure. My wife was planning to work at least another two years, my home projects were about done, and I was desiring to work at least until she retired. The job offered lots of freedom, job satisfaction, and great pay. It lasted more than a few months. One year later, I was still working, and we had that much nicer motor home paid for. Once again, the Lord had given us the desires of our heart.

The desire of our heart could be to become a missionary or an engineer. As we serve Him, He will direct our path.

DOING GOOD UNTO OTHERS

PSALMS 37:3, 27

Irate customers are just irate?

Every day, we get to make numerous choices on how we do unto others.

While I was working in the northern part of New York State, an irate customer was transferred to me in the engineering department. Before passing on the call to me, the front office receptionist said that this elderly lady was a frequent caller who liked to complain about her bill but now was complaining about electrical interference on her television. On the other end of the line, I heard an elderly lady that was very upset. She said that she could not watch her television, and she was convinced it was the electric company's fault. I listened and listened and listened for she had a lot to say. I knew that I would not be able give her a satisfactory answer at that time, so we agreed upon a time we could meet at her property.

Upon arrival, I saw a gray, small two-bedroom trailer that was at least forty years old. Inside, she sat on one of the few pieces of furniture, viewing a television that had also seen its better days. Again, I listened to her story of how the electric lines were in the wrong place, and it was causing interference reception on her television. We went out behind the trailer to take a look at the antenna and discovered the real problem. The

What is the real problem?

antenna had seen too many wind, snow, and ice storms. There was next to nothing left of it. I explained that this was not the utility company's problem, but somehow, the words did not sink in. I told her I would do a little more investigating and get back to her.

How often should we follow His leading?

At home, I spoke with my wife, and we agreed that we could do some good for this poor elderly lady. The next Saturday, we purchased a new antenna and installed it for her. I stopped by a couple more times in the next month or so and made sure she was viewing her favorite shows. She was so grateful that she offered me one of her only possessions, an old single shot .22 rifle, but I declined. A few months later, the front office receptionist that had transferred the call to me said that she never heard from the lady again about her high bills. This lady really just needed someone to talk to and made to feel like someone cared. I wish I could say I always responded to the leading of the Lord in like

So often in the corporate business world, people do wrong or evil just to try and make themselves look good. The Bible speaks of them in Psalms 37:1: "Fret not thyself because of evildoers, neither be thou envious against the workers of iniquity." So many people have the "be sure to rub elbows with the big shots and ignore those below you on the corporate ladder" attitude. This is man's wisdom, but God's wisdom tells us a completely different ways to prosper:

Why should I do good?

- "Labor not to be rich: cease from thine own wisdom." —Proverbs 23:4
- "Commit thy works unto the Lord, and thy thoughts shall be established." —Proverbs 16:3

- "By mercy and truth iniquity is purged: and by the fear of the Lord men depart from evil. When a man's ways please the Lord, he maketh even his enemies to be at peace with him." —Proverbs 16:6–7
- "If ye then, being evil, know how to give good gifts unto your children, how much more shall your Father which is in heaven give good things to them that ask him? Therefore all things whatsoever ye would that men should do to you, do ye even so to them." —Matthew 7:11–12a

Sticking with Psalms 37, let's look at three words from verse 3: "Trust in the LORD, and do good; so shalt thou dwell in the land, and verily thou shalt be fed." According to this verse, it is not enough to trust in the Lord because it goes on to say and do good. Jesus wants evidence of that trust. At work, we show the evidence of God living in us as we show good. If someone is in need, we should be the first ones there to help. If the customer is crying for help, we should do our best to be at their side. Psalms 37:27, which states, "Depart from evil, and do good; and dwell for evermore," also reminds us that we are to do good.

You think I should do my job how?

The New Testament even teaches us that we need to do good to our bosses no matter how they treat us.

- "Servants, be subject to your masters with all fear; not only to the good and gentle, but also to the froward." —1 Peter 2:18
- "Let as many servants as are under the yoke count their own masters worthy of all honour, that the name of God and his doctrine be not blasphemed." —1 Timothy 6:1
- "Exhort servants to be obedient unto their own masters, and to please them well in all things." — Titus 2:9a

I should respond to my boss how?

At least a couple different times, my bosses came to me and gave me a good chewing out. I listened and calmly told them that I understood and would be sure to take corrective action. I also told them my goal was to exceed their expectations in all my work goals and all they had to do was let me know person to person if something needed to change. They did not need to treat me like a child that they needed to get my attention by yelling. Just simply tell me what I did wrong. I requested that one supervisor not use our Savior's name in vain. Afterward, one supervisor apologized, and the other supervisor said he would be more aware of his language in the future.

An important thing to remember: the boss is in charge, and he gets to make the decisions. Having been on both sides of decision-making has made it easier to understand and then communicate that truth to both supervisor and subordinates.

As a subordinate, I made numerous suggestions to improve operations. As a supervisor, I heard and implemented even more suggestions. One of the most satisfying parts of the work environment was being part of an implemented idea but always giving credit to the originator. When one of your great ideas does not get implemented, remember what it says in Titus 2:9a: "Exhort servants to be obedient unto their own masters."

Often, Christians are not recognized for their effort in the work place. However, the Apostle Paul told us we must persist in doing the right thing. He then reminds us that our reward is one of an eternal inheritance. He also says if we do wrong, we may get away with it for a season, but ultimately, there will be appropriate consequences. Colossians

3:22–25 states, "Servants, obey in all things your masters according to the flesh; not with their eyes, as men pleasers; but in singleness of heart, fearing God; And whatsoever ye do, do it heartily, as to the Lord, and not unto men; Knowing that of the Lord ye shall receive the reward of the inheritance: for ye serve the Lord Christ. But he that doeth wrong shall receive for the wrong which he hath done: and there is no respect of persons."

How long can I get away with doing it my way?

Human nature tells us to please ourselves and impress others. This scripture tells us to do it for the Lord. Our reward for serving him is forever; most earthly rewards are satisfying at the time, but are soon forgotten.

Yes, do good things, but do them for the Lord.

PRAYING FOR GUIDANCE: WAITING ON THE LORD

PSALMS 37:7, 34

When you go to one of the seminars put on by your company, you are not likely to hear any suggestion that you should wait on the Lord or pray for guidance. We know that we should pray without ceasing, but how often do we think we know it all and go it alone instead? If you are anything like me, you get comfortable in the job and forget who got you where you are. The apostle Paul wrote in Colossians 1:15–18, "Who is the image of the invisible God, the firstborn of every creature: For by him were all things created, that are in heaven, and that are in earth, visible and invisible, whether they be thrones, or dominions, or principalities, or powers: *all things were created by him, and for him:* and he is before all things, and by him all things consist. And he is the head of the body, the church: who is the beginning, the firstborn from the dead; that in all things he might have the preeminence" (emphasis mine).

Is it legal to pray at work?

After much prayer and discussion with my wife at the age of thirty, I made the move from hourly to salary with the vision of becoming resident engineer within five years. It meant moving our family of five away from most of our extended family and from familiar surroundings. I thought that within a couple years, I would move to first

God put him in charge?

line supervisor and, then naturally, to resident engineer. The Lord, the One who is truly in charge, had other plans. It was closer to four years before I was promoted to first line supervisor in the engineering department. I had my plan, but the Lord had his. Psalms 37:34 states, "Wait on the Lord, and keep his way, and he shall exalt thee to inherit the land: when the wicked are cut off, thou shalt see it." But then the job I desired became available, and within eleven months from becoming a first line supervisor at the age of thirty-five, I was resident engineer.

What do you mean this job was a gift from above?

To get that job was a gift from above. I was one of five or six candidates, including two very qualified senior supervisors at the location that I had moved to. I knew that only by God's grace did I get that job. He does promise that if we trust him, do good, and commit our ways, He will give us the desires of our heart. True evidence of that promise was revealed at that time in my life.

Who put him in charge?

Before I started working with the other two supervisors as their supervisor, I did a lot of praying for wisdom on how to do the best job in this new position. I knew it would be a challenge since these men knew more about the job and area than I did. Using the world's thought process, it would have been easy to think that I was picked for this job, and they needed to listen to me. But Proverbs 3:5b says, "Lean not unto thine own understanding." Instead, one of the first things I did was to get these two men aside and let them know that I was glad to be selected for the job but realized they could have just as well gotten the job. I told them what my expectations were from them but more importantly that I was going to lean on their expertise and that it would be a team effort. I believe the Lord gave me the right words to bring this team together, and we were able to accomplish significant work in the next six years as we worked together.

All that matters is what I get out of my job?

But what happened during those years will have an everlasting effect. When we made that first move away from our family and started attending a small church near our new home, our family participated in the AWANA program: our three children in the program and my wife and I working as helpers. All three of our children accepted Christ as their savior during the time we attended that church. I learned more truths and promises as we studied the book of Proverbs. Our next move was to the north country of New York. While attending that church, we were able to help start an AWANA program that continued long after our short twelve-month stay there. The next move was to the Catskills, and the Lord blessed us again by being a part of their AWANA program, which had as many as ninety students attending on Friday evenings. Our kids memorized a lot of God's Word during those year, and they are serving him today—an answer to the desire of my heart.

Here is another promise from Proverbs 22:6, "Train up a child in *the way he should go:* and when he is old, he will not depart from it" (emphasis mine). Making sure our children are trained should be our number one priority. Having a job is necessary and should provide great satisfaction in our life, but we need to make sure our children are trained in the way they should go. As we wait on the Lord, He will show us how to make that happen.

Why do my kids need me around as long as I bring home the bacon?

No, we cannot see the future, but we can ask for guidance and wait on the Lord, and before we know it, we are retired and passing on some of those experiences.

LISTENING, THINKING, THEN ACTING

PSALMS 37:8

You think listening is communication?

Almost every adult education course that deals with the development of personnel has a section on communication. It might be on how to project yourself, how to write, how to deal with others, how to deal with a difficult employee, how to be sure you are understood, how to understand body language, how to ask the right questions, and the list goes on and on. The most valuable part of any of those courses is the part that explains how to communicate by listening. Thousands of years ago, Solomon was passing on that wisdom in Proverbs 18:13: "He that answereth a matter before he heareth it, it is folly and shame unto him."

Almost that long ago when I was in my senior year of high school (maybe not quite that long), I learned that very lesson from my sister who is two years younger. We had moved from Arizona to Utah about six weeks into my senior year of high school. I was not a strong communicator and definitely not very confident around girls other than my sisters. One girl that was in my sister's sophomore class had the biggest brown eyes that I had ever seen, and I had a crush on her

Why should I listen to my younger sister?

but never said anything to my sisters and for sure not this young lady. This sister told me a couple times about other girls that maybe would like to get to know me, but the feeling was not mutual, and I told her not to bother me about girls in her class. After graduation, I was talking with my sister, and she happened to mention something about the girl in her class with the big brown eyes. She replied, "Oh, she told me she liked you also, but you told me not to bother you about my classmates." After that, I let people speak their mind and listened intently.

What happens when I do not have time to listen?

Listening is critical to effective communication. Effective listening means that you not only hear, but understand what the person is saying and why they are saying it. Only then can you respond effectively. Only then will an irate person stop and listen to what you say in response to their problem or concern.

It is a good idea to pause and think before you jump into your response. That pause gives your brain a chance to review what has been said and possibly help you come up with an even clearer and a more understanding response. It also can help the other person understand that you are thinking about their situation.

Cows have feelings too?

Shortly after getting my dream job as operating superintendent, the engineering department came to me with a problem that they were having with a very upset farmer. His cows were not producing the amount of milk that they had been, and he was convinced it was the electric company's fault. The cows were not drinking from the water source in the barn. He had been told it was because of stray voltage (cows are much more sensitive to low voltage than humans). He had even had some other experts tell him that it was the electric company's problem. The engineering department had done a thorough investigation and determined that it was not a stray voltage problem coming from the electric company power lines.

After introductions were made, I was able to get the farmer aside as he started to explain why it was the electric company's fault that he was about to lose his livelihood. I listened empathetically as he told how much his cows had produced in the past and how he had done his best to keep the bills paid as the cows gave less and less milk. The cows refused to drink from the water source, and he had been told by experts that it was in fact due to stray voltage coming from the electric power lines. He even explained how another farmer had had the same problem and it was resolved by the electric company fixing their lines. I was able to get in a few comments and questions, but mostly, I just listened. I told him that I understood. I explained that I grew up on a farm and I had dealt with similar problems in the past working as an employee of the electric utility, no one wants to lose his livelihood, cows are very sensitive about stray voltage, and that it sounded like his cows were responding to a voltage problem.

How much listening is necessary?

At one point in the conversation, I could see that we were communicating—I listening to him and he to me. Only then was I able to explain how the engineering department had done their checks to determine there was no stray voltage coming from the power company lines. Only then would he listen to some additional investigating within his facilities. We were then able to determine exactly where the source of the stray voltage was coming from within his own facilities.

Too often, we get defensive when speaking with an upset person as they lash out at anyone that will pretend to listen to them. They often direct their anger at the person they feel is responsible for their frustration. Our key verse for the study is Psalms 37:8, which says, "Cease from anger, and forsake wrath: fret not thyself in any wise to do evil." I am convinced that anger shuts down our thoughts for reasoning or logic. Anger in the work place seldom ends with good results. The Bible has over 220 references to anger, but only five of those are in the New Testament.

Colossians 3:8 states, "But now ye also put off all these; *anger*, wrath, malice, blasphemy, filthy communication out of your mouth," (emphasis mine). This is a good summary of those New Testament instruction and lets us know there is no place for anger in our Christian walk. Paul tells us in the verses preceding that anger should be a thing of the past as far as our communications are concerned. Paul is not teaching us that anger is a sin. He is saying that how we react to anger can be sin as he gives us more details in Ephesians 4:26–27: "Be ye angry, and sin not: let not the sun go down upon your wrath: Neither give place to the devil."

I do not have a right to respond in anger?

This is contrary to the thinking of this world. In one of my first yearly reviews, my supervisor told me that I needed to get angry and show more emotion. The world teaches us that anger is a display of power or disgust with the other person's ideas. My guide book for how to live tells me that was not good advice. Following the instructions of the Bible has proven much more effective.

The words we use to respond are the least important part of communication. How we say those words conveys even more information. Body language tells more than the word or the inflection of our speech. The following are just a few of the things that we can communicate via body language.

You think you can read me?

- Friendly feelings
- Approval
- Deep thought
- Desire to interrupt
- Frustration
- Disapproval or rejection
- Defensive feelings
- Superiority
- Desire to delay or defer

- Ignore others
- Boredom

Why would I want to listen to you?

Back when I first started with the electric and gas utility, when an employee reached a milestone of twenty, twenty-five, thirty, etc., years of service, they were taken to lunch by their supervisors. At the age of thirty-four and at my first such luncheon outing with an employee who had thirty-five years of service, I witnessed a great example of body language. There was an employee with thirty-five years of service sitting at the table with his arms folded and his legs crossed at the feet, making short polite responses to the comments or questions of the four supervisors that had taken advantage of the free lunch he had earned. As the questions got a little more about his life as an employee, his arms relaxed at his side. As those questions continued, he became even more relaxed and leaned back in his chair. By the end of the meal, his body was totally relaxed as he lay back in his chair with open arms and his feet uncrossed. Just as if he was at home relaxing and watching his favorite television program. He was happy to explain how he had contributed to the company all those years, even before I was born.

Listening, thinking, and then acting has probably been the most rewarding part of heavenly focused work habits. I enjoyed the challenge of resolving the irate customers' concerns, listening to an employee who had a valid concern that no one wants to resolve, or hearing a great idea on how to improve productivity and helping get it implemented.

How do you get to the root of the problem?

When I returned to the division office where I started my career after seventeen years in five other locations within the company, I was put in charge of the division health and safety committee. For the past several years, that division had been near the bottom when compared to the other twelve divisions. The committee met monthly and discussed recent injuries and motor vehicle accidents. After listening for a few months, it was obvious that the rules for what was considered a "chargeable accident" was known to some on the committee, but few, if anyone beyond that, did. Some of the injuries that happened were so minor that, if reported properly, they would not have had to be chargeable. After thinking about the problem, I suggested that we communicate what was chargeable and not changeable via a message from the supervisors. Then we posted the information in a simple format on the bulletin boards. That simple message was a big part of the reason we were the top division for next three years in a row, a feat hadn't been done before or since. Eventually, that simple message was posted in all of the divisions.

Listening is the key to communication, and the most effective leaders do it best.

STAYING FOCUSED

PSALMS 37:23, 24

When is it time to throw in the towel?

One of the most challenging projects that I helped coordinate involved designing, testing, and implementing a new multimillion-dollar computer system for coordinating electric outages. The team was under tight time constraints and constant reviews and critique from upper management. Every week brought new challenges including programming or hardware problems and complaints on what was designed compared to how the users envisioned the system should work. The other project lead took care of the technical portions while I represented the user side of the system. Almost every day, we discussed concerns, and almost every month for the duration of the two-year project, there seemed to be obstacles bigger than any solution. One particular day, the other project lead said it was time to throw in the towel. I had trusted the Lord to help us get this project completed. That particular day, I used listening and reasoning skills to find yet another solution. We eventually prevailed in completing the project on time and under budget, establishing a system that proved effective and is now being used by other electric utilities.

Psalms 37:23, 24 states, "The steps of a good man are ordered by the Lord: and he delighted in his way. Though he fall, he shall not be utterly cast down: for the LORD upholdeth him with his hand."

It would have been very easy to give up on that project, but I continued to be confident and stay focused. I know that the Lord had not promised to complete the project but to give me the desires of my heart if I trusted him. The Lord is looking out for believers. If we fall, we have his promise to keep us from hitting the floor. In Psalms 18:16–18 and 2 Samuel 22:19–20, the Bible states almost the same words: "They prevented me in the day of my calamity: but the Lord was my stay. He brought me forth also into a large place: *he delivered me*, because he delighted in me" (emphasis mine). "The Lord rewarded me according to my righteousness: according to the cleanness of my hands hath *he recompensed me*. For I have kept the ways of the LORD, and have not wickedly departed from my God" (emphasis mine).

Who is going to carry you?

Notice how each passage reminds us that the Lord delights in our persistence to stay the course. In fact, when we put our trust in him, he keeps us focused. He is leading the way as it tells us in Psalm 23:3, "He restoreth my soul: he leadeth me in the paths of righteousness for his name's sake." Do not miss this point: if we stay focused on putting

When do I get some rest?

him first, he will lead us. Why? For his glory.

It is very easy to forget the reason God created us. It is very easy to lose our focus on him and focus on ourselves. It is very easy to follow the crowd. It is very easy to slip into the ways of the world. It is very easy to let Satan lead us astray. It takes a continuous effort to glorify God in all we do and say. It means that we "Live such good lives among the pagans that, though they accuse you of doing wrong, they may see your good deeds and glorify God on the day he visits us" (1 Peter 2:12). The effort that is required is much easier if we follow what Paul tells us in Romans 15:5 and 6: "May the God who gives endurance and encouragement give you a spirit of unity among yourselves as you follow Christ Jesus, so that with one heart and mouth you may glorify the God and Father of our Lord Jesus Christ."

Where is you focus?

Believers all fall. We all fall short of God's glory. How often we fall and how far we fall depends on how centered our lives are on following Christ's teaching. It should be easy to follow Christ at church. However, the work environment is the place that we often fail. God's promise is that he will not let us hit the bottom (Psalms 37:24). Instead, he will hold us up.

Changing jobs can often be a big challenge. After some big changes at the utility company I worked for, I was assigned a new job in the corporate office. My new boss gave me an assignment and a week later stopped in my office to see how I was progressing. I gave him and update, and he said, "Wow, that is way ahead of where I thought you would be. The last guy who worked on this project did not get that far in a month." When I took on that new assignment, I had asked God to keep me focused not on what I had lost in my old job but on doing my best in the new job. He honored that prayer, and I did my best to glorify Him.

Staying focused on Christ is paramount to living for Him.

CONTROLLING THE TONGUE

PSALMS 37:30

Who has the best solutions?

Toward the end of my career at the electric and gas utility, I was assigned a group that was "out of control." I had known most of these men for twenty-five years, but had not worked directly with them for over twenty. My recollection of them was that they were a good bunch of guys. However, now

I was no longer their peer, but their supervisor. Before having our first meeting, I asked for wisdom from on high. I asked of them just two things: to work safely and be productive. I promised them I would be there for them if they just did those two things to the best of their ability. They assured me that was what they always do.

It was not long until I got a call from my supervisor about one of the crews taking too long to restore power. The supervisor was not happy. Twenty-five miles away from the outage, the main office had determined what was wrong, and they knew how long it should take to do the fix. I followed up with the crew, only to be questioned by them in an angry and loud voices as to why I was questioning what had happened. Calmly, I confirmed that I believed they know what they were doing, so they just have to give me the facts so that I can explain what really happen to those that

Don't you think I know what I am doing?

think they know and jumped to the conclusion that it took too long. They did, and I reported back with the fact that the job was much more involved than they had assumed. This was repeated several times to the point that I was even accused of protecting the crews.

We know more about this. What makes you think you know more?

Another time, when I was out of the office for the day, I had assigned the work for the day, but some scheduling conflict made it impossible for the crew to do it that day. The man in charge tried several different things to overcome the conflict, but when he could not resolve it, he called the main office. There was more discussion at the main office with a conclusion that the crew was just trying to get out of the work for the day. The next day after discussion with the man in charge, my conclusion was that the crew had done what they could. I also told them that they could and should make the decision on their own and not involve the main office from that point forward. I never had that problem again. Just a simple discussion stopped the gossip and second-guessing.

There were numerous examples of how the history of not controlling the tongue between those two offices took me five years to gain the confidence of all nine or ten employees in that office. Although there were a couple of those ten employees that did not participate, we had several one-direction shouting matches about how management was misusing them. To the best of my ability and with God's leading, I strived to follow Psalms 37:30, which states, "The mouth of the righteous speaketh wisdom, and his tongue talketh of judgment." No wisdom ever came from this simple minded person, but this simple minded person is righteous because of Christ and can claim that promise each and every day. Once again, Solomon gave us some similar wisdom passed on to him from

What are you some kind of a wise guy?

the creator in Proverbs 11:12, 13: "He that is void of wisdom despiseth his neighbour: but a man of understanding holdeth his peace. A talebearer revealeth secrets: but he that is of a faithful spirit concealeth the matter."

Wisdom and controlling the tongue normally go hand in hand. James 3 might read something like this if we were to relate it to our place of work.

> Coworkers, as your boss, the buck stops here. If you make a mistake, I have not done my job in teaching you how to do your job. If I make a mistake or step on your toes, please let me know. My goal, by God's grace, is to keep you informed so that does not happen. I never talk behind your back, so if you happen to make a mistake, I will speak directly with you and would appreciate the same

You say you never get a break?

in return. I understand that what I say affects the whole department.

You will earn a reputation based on what you say—good or bad. The person known for their wisdom is not the person that constantly finds fault with his job or coworkers. They are the ones that people are attracted to for the right answers. People sense they are different. On the other hand, the godless person is more likely to harbor bitterness, and their life is full of strife and confusion. Godly wisdom brings peace to a person. A godly person is also someone who is fair in his or her dealings with coworkers. Their peace comes from God's leading in their life.

How can I get some of that peace?

What do you mean I should keep my mouth shut?

Gossip is spoken against numerous times in the Bible. It tells us that nothing can ruin your testimony quicker that a loose tongue. James 1:26 states, "If any man among you seem to be religious, and *bridleth not his tongue*, but deceiveth his own heart, this man's religion is vain" (emphasis mine). Peter tells us in his first book that if we are going to say something about another person we should keep it positive. First Peter 3:10 states, "For he that will love life, and see good days, let him refrain his tongue from evil, and his lips that they speak no guile," or as my mother taught me, "If you cannot say something good, don't say anything at all."

PUTTING HIS WAYS FIRST

PSALMS 37:31

Have you ever made the wrong choice?

Working as an electrician in industry prior to working for the electric and gas utility, I made a mistake that I tried never to repeat. Two other electricians and I were sent to a three-day school on electrical relays that was several hours away from our workplace. We were given a blank check (no receipt needed) as far as what we spent for food. I remember the first night getting a good meal, but I was still hungry and wanted seconds. When the waitress asked if I wanted anything else, I said sure, the same thing I just had. She was a little surprised, but did return with a second plate of food. Now this happened to be a bar and restaurant. The other two guys had ordered drinks with their meal, but I had a testimony to uphold and did not partake until they ordered a second time, and I said to myself, "Nobody will know the difference, and I want these guys to think I am cool." So instead of doing the right thing, I did the cool thing. I ruined my testimony with those guys, and no doubt, they carried that information back to the rest of the crews that I worked with.

Who is more important? I or me?

You see at that moment, I got the best of me. Instead of following what Psalms 37:31 says, "The law of his God is in his heart; none of his steps shall slide," my heart was full of me instead of the Holy Spirit. I let sin in and down I slid. The desire of my heart was not focused on him, but instead on me. My steps slid, and I became a stumbling block to those nonbelievers. Since that time, I have had scores of times to do the same. But I am not even comfortable during "happy hours" as I sip on a soda or nothing at all.

Paul gave us direction on how to put His ways first and how to avoid being a stumbling block in 2 Corinthians 6:3. "We put no stumbling block in anyone's path, so that our ministry will not be discredited." Much of the world has an image of "very religious" as those that do not drink alcohol. In fact growing up in a very conservative Christian home there were lots of thou shall nots such as no alcohol, no dancing, no smoking, that were not part of the Ten Commandments. The sin was not the alcohol but the fact that I had discredited the ministry.

God gave us a further explanation of right and wrong as believers through Paul's writing in 1 Corinthians 10:23-24, 31-33: "Everything is permissible—but not everything is beneficial. Everything is permissible—but not everything is constructive. Nobody should seek his own good, but the good of others. So whether you eat or drink or whatever you do, do it all for the glory of God. Do not cause anyone to stumble, whether Jews, Greeks or the church of God—even as I try to please everybody in every way. For I am not seeking my own good but the good of many, so that they may be saved."

What is the difference between your right and my wrong?

Something most of use learned as children in church is how to get JOY. Put Jesus first, Others second, and Yourself last. His way first, the good of others second, and our desires last. What is not normally taught in that lesson is that by putting Christ first and others second not only do we get joy but as the last part of verse I Corinthians 10:33 says others will be saved.

Whether a coworker is a peer, supervisor or subordinate, if they are nonbelievers, they will know if we are treating them the way they believe a Christian should treat others. If we are honest or dishonest, fair or unfair, respectful or disrespectful, they know if we are putting His ways first. Not until we get to heaven will we know how many nonbelievers we were able to influence to the point of them accepting Christ as their Savior.

How can I make this tough decision?

The first part of Psalms 37:31 says, "The law of his God is in his heart." Obviously, in order to get his law in our heart, we need to be studying his Word, praying, and attending a Bible-preaching and teaching church. A verse I memorized as a boy still sticks with me today: "Study to show thyself approved unto God, a workman that needeth not to be ashamed, rightly dividing the word of truth" (II Timothy 2:15). The more we study and understand the Scripture, the less likely we are to end up being ashamed. The more we study, the better we are equipped to do our job as we know the right direction to turn when tough decisions come our way.

"But by the grace of God I am what I am: and his grace which was bestowed upon me was not in vain; but I laboured more abundantly than they all: yet not I, *but the grace of God which was with me*" (1 Corinthians 15:10, emphasis mine). This verse reminds us that we have to let God do the work. Again, this happens when we truly put his ways first. Let him work through us.

One of the last days of my career at the electric utility, I had lunch with the crew with which I had spent the last ten years. I offered each of them a New Testament, explaining that they did not have to take one. Each one did take it and said thanks. I am reminded that we need not be ashamed of the gospel as we put His ways first in our lives.

BEING AT PEACE

PSALMS 37:11, 37

Can a salad boy be at peace?

Shortly after getting married, my wife and I moved from New York to Arizona. While attending college there, I worked in the restaurant business, washing dishes, prepping a salad bar, and waiting on tables. As a salad boy, as we were called, we had access to the storage area where all supplies were kept. I had asked the supervisor if I could have one of the T-shirts from the storage area with the restaurant name on it for my wife. She was amazed that I had not already taken several. I do not claim to be perfect, except through the sacrifice of Jesus, but I do strive to do the right thing and believe it is a much more peaceful life as we are promised in Psalms 37:37: "Mark the perfect man, and behold the upright: *for the end of that man is peace*" (emphasis mine).

Can you have peace on a bad day?

Most jobs have their good and bad days. Most of us have had good and bad bosses. Most of the time at work, there are good and bad coworkers. Most of us will obtain a good or bad reputation for what we do and accomplish at work. All of us can have the peace that passes all understanding as Paul said in Philippians 4:7, "And the peace of God, which passeth all understanding, shall keep your hearts and minds through Christ Jesus." We have the promise of the second part of Psalms 37:39: "But the salvation of the righteous is of the Lord: he is their *strength in the time of trouble*" (emphasis mine). When those tough days, bad bosses, or coworkers come along, we can lean on him as we recall a scripture promise or say a prayer of guidance.

Even in the times of trouble, we have the promise of peace as it says in John 16:33: "These things I have spoken unto you, that in me ye might have peace. In the world ye shall have tribulation: but be of good cheer; I have overcome the world."

Part of being at peace is based on our attitude. Charles Swindoll summarized it this way:

> The longer I live the more I realize the impact of attitude on life. Attitude, to me, is more important than facts. It is more important than the past, than education, money, circumstances, failures, successes or what other people think or say or do. It is more important

Being a peace is a choice?

> than appearances, giftedness or skill. It will make or break a person. The remarkable thing is we have a choice every day regarding the attitude we embrace for that day. We can not change our past … we can not change the fact that people will act in a certain way. We can not change the inevitable. The only thing we can do is focus on the one thing we have, and that is that life is 10 percent what happens to me and 90 percent how I react to it. And so it is with you…you are in charge of your attitude.

It is easy to get caught up with the negative attitudes that often prevail in the workplace. So much negative about coworkers, so much dishonesty, so much jealously, so much tribulation (John 16:33) that if we believers are not leaning on Him we can get drawn into the muck as well.

Many years ago the verbal fighting between the gas and electric departments was on the rise to almost the breaking point. The gas supervisor and I, as the electric supervisor, were frequently behind closed doors with one or more employees as they complained about some minor issue that had blown up into a seemingly major problem. It would have been easy for us as supervisors to be defensive and take sides and not look at the root cause. However, as the other supervisor and I looked into each issue, they all seem to have the same root problem. Jealousness. He has or is getting something I want. It is not fair. We got the groups together and had a short meeting concluding with Charles Swindoll's statement above. Peace was restored as each one thought about the reality of those words.

You at peace?

I am thankful for the peace that is promised us from our Creator and when life's big or little issues arise, I can lean on Him and seek His peace. A peace that cannot be understood by the world.

CONCLUSION

Psalm 37:39, 40 states, "But the salvation of the righteous is of the Lord, he is their strength in the time of trouble. And the Lord shall *help* them, and *deliver* them: he shall deliver them from the wicked, and *save* them, because they trust in him" (all emphasis mine). There are three promises of what the Lord will do for the righteous in verse 40: *help them, deliver them, save them*. Why? Because of their trust in his promises. These verses also tell us he is also our strength in time of trouble. We just have to lean on him.

How can we bring Him glory?

Psalms 37, verse after verse, teaches us how to live our lives and please him. It gives us at least eight heavenly ways to please him in our lives. Applying them to our work life, family life, recreation life, or church life is going to glorify the Lord.

The choices are ours alone. We are not a puppet on a string controlled by God or his angels. He is there to help us, deliver us, and save us. We continuously make choices.

It is amazing how God directs our lives as we let him drive and put his ways first. He helps us do good to others and brings joy into our hearts at the same time. He delivers us from our selfish ways if we seek his guidance and we wait on Him. He delivers us from letting our tongue get us in trouble. He helps us communicate better if we follow His simple truths. As we stay focused on serving Him and putting His ways ahead of ours, He brings a peace into our lives that passes all human understanding.

As a teen, I really struggled with what to do with my life. The high school guidance counselor tested me and told me my strengths were in engineering. She also said I would never make it since I did not have the drive or ability that was needed. In church gatherings, we were constantly challenged to serve the Lord. It seemed to serve the Lord meant becoming a full time missionary or pastor. At age eighteen, I decided that I would go into civil engineering since I liked being outside, but did not like being around electricity and was not very mechanical. At that point in my life did I really know the exact directions God would lead me?

Who has control?

As a young adult, I continued to struggle with the answer to "what did the Lord want me to do with my life" but tried to trust Christ as my wife and I started raising our family. It took a while for me to finally get that bachelor's degree in electrical technology. There were good and bad times as we learned to lean on Him instead of our own understanding. Looking back, it is easy to see his blessings time and time again. It is also easy to see that what is really important is letting Him take control no matter what our vocation. He will lead us all the same way.

Someday we will be judged for what we did in those few short years here on earth as it says in Colossians 3:23-25: "Whatever you do, work at it with all your heart, as working for the Lord, not for men, since you know that you will receive an inheritance from the Lord as a reward. It is the Lord Christ you are serving. Anyone who does wrong will be repaid for his wrong, and there is no favoritism." When believers are judged for their dedication to serving Him each and every day, what we did at work will have a big impact on our inheritance. We want to be sure we did what his will was for our life. Yes, it starts with a foundation of:

1. Accepting him as our savior
2. Turning over (dedicate) our lives to him
3. Taking up our cross each day and follow him

We must then "wok at it with all your heart' as it says in verse 23 of Colossians 3 by following all of Christ teaching including the eight heavenly focused habits found in Psalms 37.